MARILYN
MARCH 1955

MARILYN
MARCH 1955

Photographs from The
MICHAEL OCHS ARCHIVES
by
ED FEINGERSH
Text by
BOB LaBRASCA

Delta

A Delta Book
Published by
Bantam Doubleday Dell Publishing Group, Inc.
666 Fifth Avenue
New York, New York 10103

Special thanks to Goldman/Taylor Entertainment
Company, Bob Miller, and Madeleine Morel

Book design by Robin Arzt

Library of Congress Cataloging in Publication Data

Marilyn : March 1955 / photographs by Ed Feingersh from The Michael Ochs
Archives ; text by Bob LaBrasca
p. cm.
ISBN 0-385-30119-7 : $12.95 ($15.95 Can.)
1. Monroe, Marilyn, 1926–1962—Portraits. I. Feingersh, Ed.
II. LaBrasca, Bob. III. The Michael Ochs Archives.
PN2287.M69M287   1990   90-34429
791.43'028'092—dc20   CIP

Manufactured in the United States of America
Published simultaneously in Canada
November 1990

10 9 8 7 6 5 4 3 2 1

KPP

Man is in love and loves what vanishes,
What more is there to say?

— W. B. Yeats

You can mull the anecdotal remnants of Marilyn Monroe's life and pore over her pictures, moving and still; you can give yourself up to the daydream of her curves, her wide eyes, moist lips and perpetual breathy anticipation; or you can try to plumb the psychology of a consumer nation at the peak of its unreflective adolescence and theorize about the need of a post-war capitalist society to create a barren goddess of voluptuary longing . . . and still (more than a quarter century after her chemically induced death) be left with the same bottomless riddle: Why did she—*does she*—mean so much to us? Her image looks out from the walls of art museums, from public murals, from souvenir albums and coffee mugs and the backs of playing cards, and we don't know quite why we keep staring back. To understand that we'd have to know much more about ourselves than we're willing to know: about the depth and complexity of what we—both men and women, individually and collectively—see and want in sex and in women, in the whole idea of "woman."

It's a tortuous conundrum that emanates from a volatile place in the soul, and there's no end to it. Which makes it eerie, and a little sad, finally, to recognize that at the center of it all was frail Marilyn herself, a creature with few more resources than any of us might have to deal with the bizarre role in which she was cast—though the fact is she had pursued the part with a vengeance.

Often enough, Marilyn is portrayed as the victim: Norma Jean Mortenson, a child of working-class Los Angeles, uncertain paternity, possible sexual abuse and a mother who was chronically mentally ill; shunted from a succession of foster homes to an orphanage to another foster home to the charge of a manipulative guardian, and finally to an arranged marriage when she was barely sixteen. It doesn't take a credentialed psychologist to spot this as a formula for feverish desire and perpetual frustration, for an unfulfillable search for love. But there are thousands of fractured family histories and only one Marilyn Monroe. In important ways she ruled her own life—certainly more than most of us do.

From the moment in 1944 when an army magazine photographer first spotted her working in an aircraft plant and offered her a modeling job, she began an inexorable, even ruthless, drive for the top. She may never have made money at prostitution, though she told some intimates that she did (she told others that she didn't), and she may not have had all the sexual affairs that she and various putative lovers have claimed; but there's no doubt that she slept with a great many men (and perhaps some women) helpful to her in becoming, by 1954, Hollywood's "Most Popular Actress." From early on, she had cultivated favored members of the press, who were likewise useful, and probably slept with some of them as well. She had undeniable gifts, and not just physical ones (well-formed bodies are commonplace in casting offices). There was a childlike glow about her, a strange ingenuous charisma that seduced most anyone who entered her sphere, and seduced the camera as well. And she used it, shrewdly and deliberately.

But there was a gnawing discomfort even in achieved stardom. As a contract player with Twentieth Century-Fox, Marilyn felt undercompensated and unappreciated. And the choices were limited for the paradigm sex object of mid-'50s America. The most desired woman on the planet, she doubted that she was worth having and sought always to "improve" herself. She read books by Emerson, Whitman, Poe, Proust, Wolfe and Joyce. She sought the company of older, sophisticated men who could teach her the true ways of the world, while in picture after picture she played out the public role of the well-endowed fluffdoll.

Her ascension to the stratospheric reaches of popular culture culminated in 1954, the year she married "Joltin' Joe" DiMaggio, the absolute hero of working-class male America, a man whose legend would enshrine him not only in the Hall of Fame but in literature and popular song. It was all too dizzyingly perfect: the orphan girl, the apple-cheeked defense plant cover model, Miss Cheesecake, the most American of movie sex queens, in union with the son of a fisherman, the broad-shouldered swinger of the big bat, the wholesome king of the Great American pastime. This was a marriage not of individuals but of national deities.

And it was doomed: Marilyn, the unregenerate exhibitionist, the woman/child libertine, cringed and rebelled against Joe's naive possessiveness and old-world jealousy. They were wed in mid-January, and their painful struggle would come to a dramatic watershed in New York City in September—in that indelible scene during the shooting of *The Seven Year Itch,* with Marilyn standing on the subway grating with wind machines blasting her skirt to her shoulders, exposing her legs and pantied bottom to all the world, while Joe watched from the wings in embarrassed rage. In the volatile aftermath Marilyn left him and, by the end of October, had secured a divorce.

But even that wasn't the end of it. On November 5, DiMaggio, his goombah Frank Sinatra and a pair of apparently incompetent private detectives in DiMaggio's employ executed the infamous "Wrong Door Raid," the break-in of an apartment on Waring Avenue in Hollywood. They expected to find Marilyn in the arms of another man but succeeded only in terrifying the apartment's tenant. (Meanwhile, upstairs and within earshot, Marilyn and the man into whose arms she had momentarily fled apparently sat quietly, witnessing the whole sordid hubbub.)

These months were chaotic and certainly a miserable time for Marilyn. Not more than two days after the Wrong Door Raid, she entered Cedars of Lebanon Hospital (chauffeured there personally by Joe) for "corrective female surgery." Whether this was an abortion or perhaps an operation for the endometriosis from which she suffered is not known, but it can only have been a dark experience, as her decaying relationship with DiMaggio lingered on despite the divorce.

By the end of 1954, reeling from these defeats and intrusions, and further bludgeoned by unanimously sneering reviews of her performance in the recently released *There's No Business Like Show Business*, she fled L.A. for rural Connecticut in the company of her soon-to-be-more-visible confidant and business advisor, photographer Milton Greene. They had met a year and a half earlier when Greene, on assignment from *Look* magazine, came West for a photo session with Marilyn. From the first he'd been a sympathetic ear, sensitive to her complaints of financial and artistic mistreatment by the studio, and he was interested in photographing her in a more casual, less stagy fashion than she was used to. Greene had his own dreams of producing respectable independent films, and he and Marilyn commiserated often about their respective ambitions. Now they were hatching a plan for Marilyn's rebirth as a legitimate actress.

Her next months were spent mostly in quiet retreat with Greene and his wife Amy at their rural home outside Weston, Connecticut. Biographers say she helped around the house, tended to the Greenes' young son Josh and read books from the Greene library—and that she took great delight in the lush coming of spring to the New England countryside. In January she and Milton Greene announced the formation of a partnership, Marilyn Monroe Productions, which would produce films independently, films that would allow Marilyn to break the studio mold of the blond sexpot and pursue her career as a serious actress. Twentieth Century-Fox asserted to anyone who'd listen that they held her under contract for another three years, but Marilyn ignored their pronouncements.

There were periodic trips from the Greenes' home to New York City, where she began psychoanalysis and met acting guru Lee Strasberg of the Actors Studio. Strasberg instinctively declared his faith in Marilyn's innate abilities and began giving her private lessons in preparation for introducing her to his regular classes. Throughout these spring months she was treated as a welcome member of the Greene family, with Milton guiding her business affairs and future plans and Amy, then a fashion model, coordinating her wardrobe and playing the role of the more settled and sensible older sister—though she was in fact half a decade younger than Marilyn.

This was a time when Marilyn seemed to relinquish the hysterical, narcissistic drive that had made her the world's most desired sex object and to embrace deeper aspirations: to survey her own inner dimensions, to earn the respect of her colleagues, to grow in her work and perhaps find a permanent soul mate. It made Hollywood nervous. *Variety* speculated whether Darryl F. Zanuck, head of Twentieth Century-Fox, would find a way to woo her back to the fold when he returned from a European vacation.

Marilyn spent the last week of March, when all of the photographs in these pages were taken, in New York City. Two public events punctuated that week: the New York opening of Tennessee Williams's *Cat on a Hot Tin Roof* at the Morosco Theater, which Marilyn would attend flanked by the Greenes on March 24; and a star-studded benefit performance of the Ringling Bros. Barnum & Bailey Circus, organized by show-biz tycoon Mike Todd, at Madison Square Garden on March 30—when Marilyn was to make her grand entrance atop a pink elephant.

Throughout the week Marilyn would be shadowed by Ed Feingersh, a photographer from a New York photo agency working on assignment for *Redbook* magazine. Feingersh's work as a New York photojournalist is not widely remembered, but he was obviously a man of substantial gifts, inspired by Marilyn as a subject and by the exceptional access he was given. No doubt his portfolio had been seen and approved by Milton Greene, himself a highly respected photographer who had now taken on the duties of image maker. Allowing Feingersh the freedom to follow her closely and shoot candidly was clearly a calculated gamble on Greene's part—that the beauty he saw in Marilyn would come through even without attentive makeup artists, wardrobe experts and glamorous lighting. Through Feingersh's gritty sensitivity Greene obviously hoped to provide Marilyn with the fully human public presence she had so far been denied.

(Some of Feingersh's images would be printed in a July 1955 *Redbook* spread entitled "The Marilyn Monroe You've Never

Seen." Later, those shots, and all outtakes, negatives and contact sheets, were filed away and ultimately hauled off to a New York warehouse where they moldered until late 1987 when archivist Michael Ochs purchased them as part of a larger lot of unexamined material.)

The vast majority of thousands of previous photographs of her had depicted not Marilyn the person but Marilyn the confection — a commodity synthesized by publicists and Hollywood businessmen devoted to keeping the sex-cash flowing and maximizing their share of the take. To humanize Marilyn would have been to betray the showmanship of glamour that was their stock-in-trade. The photographs in these pages are of a different Marilyn, a Marilyn who has ended a tumultuous marriage, declared her independence from the Hollywood maelstrom, and who now faces a world of fresh and hopeful possibilities. Greene understood the mystique of glamour, but saw its pitfalls as well. It's telling that some of these pictures were taken in the subway (specifically the Grand Central Station stop of the Lexington Avenue line). They were posed: Marilyn never used public transportation at this point in her life — she had, after all, one of the most recognizable faces in the world — but the intended message was clear: "Marilyn Monroe is just another struggling actress, a working girl."

The majority of these images were not fabricated or posed. Feingersh followed Marilyn and the Greenes through final primping for the *Cat on a Hot Tin Roof* premiere. Later, at El Morocco, he'd catch Milton Berle bending her ear. (Marilyn had known him since their meeting on the set of *Ladies of the Chorus* in 1949; he has claimed for the record, at least once, that he had an affair with her then.) He shot her at ease in her hotel room, on a rooftop and at a side table in Costello's restaurant.

Feingersh's eye had a field day at Brooks Costume, where Marilyn was fitted for the circus gala. (According to at least one biography, she burst into tears in the course of the pinning and pawing.) Milton Greene was at her side throughout to reassure her and approve the final ensemble — that's him in the lower foreground of one photo looking up at Marilyn, whose image is reflected behind him in a mirror. James Stroock, the white-haired proprietor of the costume shop, oversaw the operation, assisted by Mary Smith, his best fitter. The tall, thin, dark-haired man present at the fitting and seen with Marilyn in several other situations is Dick Shepherd, then an agent heading up MCA's motion picture department in New York (later an executive for a succession of studios and the producer of several important films; currently one of the owner/partners of the Artists Agency). Shepherd remembers

MCA's mission as "endeavoring to counteract the refrigeration that she'd been subjected to by Fox at the time. They felt they could enjoin her from working." Marilyn, he recalls, was "deadly serious about the work she wanted to do."

Also present at the Brooks Costume fitting was a United Press reporter named H. D. Quigg, now retired. When a sampling of these photographs was the subject of a special issue of *L.A. Style* magazine in February 1988, Quigg, who appeared in one of the pictures but was not identified (he is the man with glasses and dark, curly hair), wrote the publication, recalling the events of the day in colorful detail:

". . . they announced there would be a press event (opportunity?) at the Monroe fitting for the circus costume that she would howdah in. The ETA for Miss Monroe was ten or ten-thirty A.M.—I forget which after thirty-three years—but of course Monroe didn't show . . . the entrance corridor was enthronged with the press, most prominently with television spielers and paraphernalia flunkies and their impedimenta.

"Before noon, it became apparent she was reluctant to face a mob, so the media began departing. The proprietor of the place came over to me and said, 'Why don't you come back at about two?' I don't know why he picked me, unless I looked sedate, but anyhow I wasn't a mob.

"At two P.M. I arrived and the proprietor was there, and shortly the elevator arrived bearing Miss Monroe and her manager, Milt Greene. So without a word we proceeded through the place, through ladies in mid-costume oohing and aahing at the celebrity, to a trying-on cubicle. There, with what seemed to me to be remarkable dispatch, Miss Monroe got undressed to stark naked. . . .

"Since I didn't really know what I was doing there, I did nothing but memorize her skin, of which there were tundras. . . . Anyhow, the seamstress arrived with the costume, knelt down, and slipped it up and on. I was not conscious of there being a photographer there, but I notice he got shots of her beginning to get undressed. She was smiling all the while I was there; certainly no tears. . . ."

On the night of the circus benefit (for the Arthritis and Rheumatism Foundation), Marilyn dressed in rooms Greene had rented at New York's old Ambassador Hotel, so that he and Amy and Marilyn could greet a few West Coast visitors. Michael Todd, always the generous host, had flown most of his guest stars into town first-class. Among them were: Jeanette MacDonald and Gene Raymond, James Cagney, Red Buttons, Martha Raye, Terry Moore, Julius LaRosa, Sammy Davis, Jr., Sonja Henie and Bess Myerson. Amy Greene had commissioned Norman Norell to design the black silk dress Marilyn would wear to the Garden and to the socializing afterwards. This was a major public appearance, Marilyn's first since leaving Los Angeles. The contested Fox contract forbade paid performances, but charity events were exempt.

Marilyn traveled with Shepherd by limousine to the Garden, where her appearance was a hungrily awaited spectacle. She managed to get inside, move through the bowels of the hall in relative privacy and get dressed. But inside the auditorium about 200 photographers jockeyed for position as she finally entered the ring; ringmaster Milton Berle had to ask them to squat down so as not to obscure the view. *Variety* reported: "[The tableau was] climaxed by Marilyn Monroe atop a painted pink pachyderm. The photogs really messed up the procession, crowding the path of the slightly clad film star in a manner that impeded progress and movement. Miss Monroe's natural attributes are hard to follow, but eventually, the crowd got over it." None of the other international stars rated more than a name mention. The night was a grand success, helping to underscore Marilyn's predominance in an industry based a continent away.

By the end of the year Milton Greene would succeed in renegotiating her contract with Fox, winning on every major point and helping to break permanently the studio's proprietary control over their stable of stars.

In May Marilyn would begin her intimacy with Arthur Miller—the most sustained romantic relationship of her life—as her skills as an actress were blooming under Strasberg's tutelage. In her remaining seven years she would make *Bus Stop, The Prince and the Show Girl, Some Like It Hot, Let's Make Love* and *The Misfits,* all of which would bring her critical praise that had been unthinkable before her flight with Greene from Los Angeles. Eventually, of course, her relationship with Greene soured in suspicion and dissolved, her obeisance to Strasberg turned to neurotic dependence, and her marriage to Miller withered before her own internal torments. But the moment captured in these pictures is the turning point toward the best chances Marilyn would ever have.

Ed Feingersh is deceased. Milton Greene died in 1985, and Marilyn was, of course, gone by the end of 1962. She's remembered as wounded, lonely, schizoid, even pathetic, but with luminous energy—magnetic and vastly enviable.

Marilyn and Manhattan: Fresh-faced and willing, she cast a contemplative gaze on the city where she'd try for a rebirth.

The sex goddess in rebellion reveled in a solitary smoke, when cigarettes were still part of a star's romantic image.

Having stepped off the Hollywood treadmill, Marilyn faced the future full of optimism and a newfound sense of independence.

It's March 24. In her suite at the Ambassador Hotel, sheathed in gold lamé, she primped for the premiere of Tennessee Williams's *Cat on a Hot Tin Roof*.

Even the face of the most desired woman in the world needed careful tending; Marilyn had mastered some of the craft of glamour.

This was to be Marilyn's first public appearance in months; the event would draw a host of celebrities and a watchful press.

Powdering and perfuming herself seemed to give Marilyn a childish joy, as if she were still at play in Mommy's boudoir.

To a reporter who'd asked what she wore to bed, Marilyn once replied, "Chanel No. 5"; she also wore it to openings.

Marilyn had a
lifelong affair with
the mirror that was
no doubt sometimes
stormy. With the
camera it was
always true love.

A clear, well-lighted face: In the glow of a makeup lamp, Marilyn touches up the lips that had come to symbolize sensuality.

Powdered, painted, scented, coiffed and draped in ermine, Marilyn was ready for a New York night on the town.

That universally admired silhouette, highlighted in gold lamé, inspired photographer Ed Feingersh's flair for composition.

The *Cat on a Hot Tin Roof* opening at the Morosco Theater: Even in this A-list audience, Marilyn had the glow of celebrity.

To her left was Greene himself, the man who had rescued Marilyn from Hollywood's special brand of glamorous servitude.

To Marilyn's right (barely visible) was one of her escorts: Amy Greene, wife of friend and business partner Milton Greene.

Greene was her trusted advisor and confidant; she never doubted, at least not yet, that he had her best interests at heart.

While some of the photos taken this week were apparently posed, others were utterly candid. This series seems to reveal a genuine intimacy between Marilyn and Greene.

After the
performance
Marilyn let herself
be waylaid for
autographs.

In the lobby she
faced the crowd
before heading off to
a dinner party at El
Morocco.

At the El Morocco party following the *Cat* premiere Marilyn basked in the warmth of benign attention. Other celebrities, many of whom had been flown in from the West Coast by Mike Todd for the gala Ringling Brothers benefit the following weekend, greeted her cordially. They were naturally curious about her progress and her plans, as she was still holding out against the contractual claims of Darryl Zanuck's 20th Century-Fox back in California. Milton "Mr. Television" Berle (whose once immensely popular *The Milton Berle Show* was about to be canceled by NBC) was among those who bent her ear. Berle, who later claimed to have had an affair with Marilyn on the set of *Ladies of the Chorus* in 1949, was to be the ringmaster at the circus gala; Marilyn would ride an elephant.

The evening having
taken its toll,
Marilyn
surrendered to
exhaustion.

On Marilyn's trips to the city from Milton and Amy Greene's Connecticut retreat, she studied at the Actors Studio, and it was not unusual for her to read serious writing about her craft.

She also stayed abreast of the trades, where her own battle with the studio powers was being diligently covered.

As part of the effort to cast her in the role of a struggling young actress, Marilyn descended into the Grand Central subway station, where these surprisingly natural shots were taken.

Accompanied by Dick Shepherd of the MCA Agency (subsequently a studio executive, now an owner/ partner of the Artists Agency), she waited for the train . . .

. . . which took
some time to arrive.

She had, however, an unaristocratic air about her and seemed almost at home among the straphangers.

Marilyn's ride on the uptown local was a definite contrivance: By 1955 she had one of the most recognizable faces on earth, and never used public transportation.

The posing over, Marilyn and Dick Shepherd returned to street level.

They stopped later at Costello's restaurant, where Marilyn admired the James Thurber drawings that decorated its walls. It had been a long day.

Back at the Ambassador, Marilyn chatted with Shepherd over drinks as Feingersh's shooting day came to a close. In these images she seems more relaxed and unselfconscious than in any of Feingersh's other photo sessions during the week. These shots give perhaps the purest glimpse of the pensive, intimate charm of which she was capable. This was the Marilyn with whom a man could feel completely at home. Shepherd recalls Marilyn as "deadly serious about the work she wanted to do."

She hit the streets later in the week for a trip to Elizabeth Arden, this time playing for a bit more glamour than in the subway session. Feingersh's compositions paint her small against the cityscape—in counterpoint to the rooftop shots, where she appears almost to command Manhattan.

In her hotel suite
she clowns for
Feingersh's camera,
flashing her patented
lascivious smile.

In midweek she presented herself at the Brooks Costume Company for a fitting of the outfit she'd wear in the circus gala on March 30. Those present included (from left): Mary Smith, the fitter; Dick Shepherd; James Stroock, the proprietor of Brooks; and H. D. Quigg, a reporter for United Press International.

Also on hand for the Stroock fitting was Milton Greene (left), whom Marilyn trusted to approve the ensemble.

Ed Feingersh made ample use of the surreal kaleidoscope of perspectives that the Brooks Costume shop mirrors provided, even catching a glimpse of himself as he shot, sandwiched between reflections of Marilyn. Members of the Brooks staff, meanwhile, watched from the wings. (Note H. D. Quigg, who would later report having seen Marilyn nude on this day, with his face now turned to a blind corner.)

The pinning, poking and pawing, the constant inspection from every conceivable angle, the tentative approval and repeated readjustments, played havoc with Marilyn's emotions. According to one witness, she was finally reduced to tears.

Marilyn seemed to enjoy getting dressed for the camera (much the way she sometimes seemed to enjoy getting undressed for it). This was March 30, the night of the circus benefit, and Amy Greene had commissioned Norman Norell to design the black silk dress she would wear to the event. With a dresser's attentive help she made the final preparations.

Throughout the limousine ride to Madison Square Garden, accompanied by Dick Shepherd, Marilyn was animated and radiant. She would be the centerpiece of the show and was prepared to shine.

She made her way inside with Shepherd at her elbow and chatted with well-wishers in the bowels of the Garden before slipping off to her dressing room to don the sequined and bustled circus costume.

A swarm of eager reporters and photographers descended as Marilyn prepared to climb aboard an elephant that had been painted pink for the occasion. A legion of top-ranked stars was participating in the benefit, but none had the media appeal of Marilyn Monroe. The great beast kneeled to receive her. She climbed aboard, and it lurched slowly forward through the sea of paparazzi toward the spotlights of the arena.

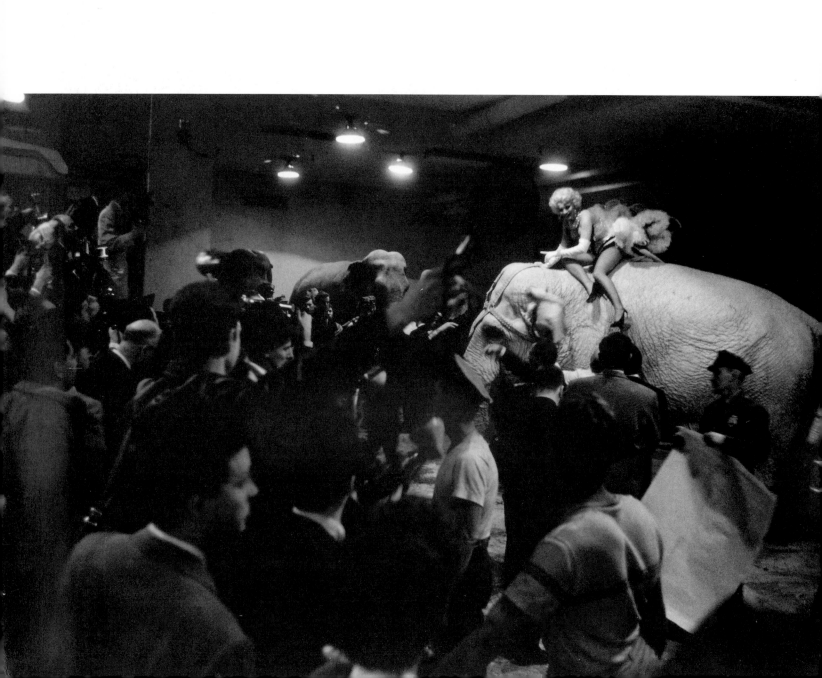

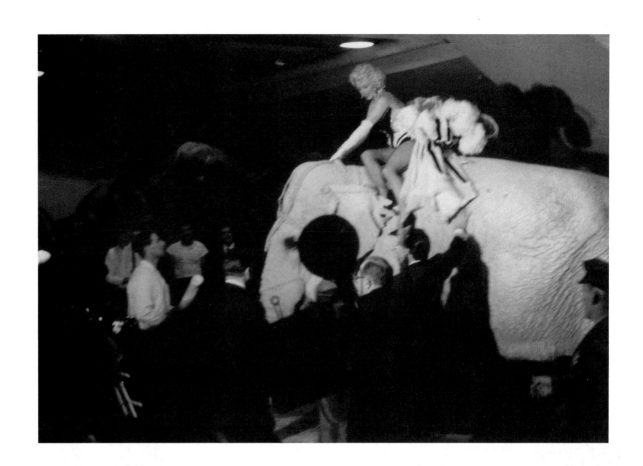